Thomas Wolsey: Henry VIII's Cardinal

A Tudor Times Insight

By Tudor Times

Published by Tudor Times Ltd

Tudor Times Insights

Tudor Times Insights are books collating articles from our website www.tudortimes.co.uk which is a repository for a wide variety of information about the Tudor and Stewart period 1485 – 1625. There you can find material on People, Places, Daily Life, Military & Warfare, Politics & Economics and Religion. The site has a Book Review section, with author interviews and a book club. It also features comprehensive family trees, and a 'What's On' event list with information about forthcoming activities relevant to the Tudors and Stewarts.

Titles in the Series

Profiles

People

Politics & Economy

Contents

Thomas Wolsey: Henry VIII's Cardinal

Introduction

Thomas Wolsey was the last, and probably the greatest, of the mediaeval ecclesiastics who wielded power in England. He rose from being the son of an Ipswich butcher, to being called the Arbiter of Europe and a credible candidate for the Papacy. Whilst he was not the first man to climb to power through the Church, he was one of the most talented, ambitious and controversial figures ever to hold a position of supreme authority under the king.

Wolsey was a byword in his own time for magnificence and extravagance. He understood the importance of spectacle and outward appearance as a tool of power and brought this to bear in his building programmes and his diplomatic triumphs.

He was a figure much hated by the king's other councillors, although his servants and colleagues seem to have been very attached to him, and there is no doubt that Henry VIII felt more personal affection for him than for the majority of his other ministers. It was not until the nineteenth century that his reputation was rehabilitated, and he was seen as a great statesman.

Henry VIII's right hand man for fifteen years, Wolsey's eventual fall was as precipitous as his rise.

Thomas Wolsey's Life Story

Chapter 1: Obscurity (1470 – 1501)

Ipswich, Suffolk, in the late 1470s was one of the most prosperous towns in England. East Anglia was an important centre of the wool trade, with English fleeces being sent from its ports to the Low Countries and goods imported in return. Within Ipswich there was a school, probably attached to one of the monasteries, where the sons of local traders and farmers could learn to read and write in English and Latin, and study enough mathematics to run a business. To this school, went a young boy by the name of Thomas Wolsey.

Thomas Wolsey's birth and parentage is not absolutely proven, but the generally accepted view is that he was born in the early 1470s to Robert Wolsey (or Wulcy) a butcher and grazier of Ipswich, and his wife Joan Daundy. It seems likely that he had an older brother, both from his name (most first sons were named for their father) and from the fact that his father was keen for him to become a priest, as evidenced by Robert Wolsey's Will. Had Thomas been the older son, he would have been expected to carry on the prosperous family business.

Thomas did so well at school that he was given one of the four scholarships in the gift of the Bishop of Norwich to Magdalen College, Oxford. His exceptional intellect enabled him to complete his BA by the age of fifteen – even in a time when many scholars completed their BA earlier than is done now, this was considered remarkable.

As with most scholars, the next step was a Fellowship of his College, followed by ordination as a priest on 10th March 1498. Later that year,

Wolsey was appointed as Master of Magdalen School, Oxford and then College Bursar in 1499. It has been alleged that whilst in his position of Bursar, he misappropriated funds - not for his own use, but for building works on the College tower. This story is plausible, given Wolsey's later penchant for building, but, according to his chief biographer, Peter Gwyn in *"The King's Cardinal"*, there is no record of it in the documents of Magdalen, and he was not deprived of his Fellowship.

Among the schoolmaster's pupils were the three sons of Thomas Grey, 2nd Marquess of Dorset, half-brother to Queen Elizabeth of York. At Christmas 1499, Wolsey was called upon to accompany the young Grey boys to their home at Bradgate in Leicestershire. He obviously impressed his host, the Marquess, and was granted a living at Limington in Somerset. Receipt of a living of the scale of Limington (£21 per annum) obliged him to resign his Fellowship. Priests were also supposed to live in their parishes, unless they had a licence to be absent.

According to his earliest biographer, his gentleman-usher, George Cavendish, Wolsey went to Limington and carried out his functions as parish priest and schoolmaster, and whilst there fell out with the local landowner, Sir Amyas Paulet, who had him set in the stocks for some misdemeanour. Later biographers have cast doubt on this, not only as it would be most unusual to shame a priest in such a manner, but also because there is some doubt as to whether Wolsey went to Limington at all. However, if the rumour were current during Wolsey's lifetime, or just after, it no doubt gave rise to a good deal of sniggering.

Chapter 2: Early Career (1501 – 1509)

There was never any possibility of a man so talented and ambitious as Wolsey living in the country and ministering to his flock. He was obviously expecting promotion, as he applied on 3 November 1500 for a Papal Licence to hold more than one living.

In 1501, presumably through the good offices of Dorset, he became Chaplain to Henry Deane, Archbishop of Canterbury, who was also Lord Keeper of The Great Seal – a crucial position in English Government, as without the Great Seal, no official business could be implemented.

Whilst in the Archbishop's household, Wolsey would have spent most of his time at Lambeth Palace, and was probably there when Katharine of Aragon stayed there in 1501, prior to being married by Archbishop Deane to Prince Arthur on 14th November 1501. The pageants for the wedding were magnificent, and this is when Wolsey may first have witnessed the power of spectacle as propaganda.

Wolsey was also in Archbishop Deane's train when he visited Scotland in negotiations related to the Treaty of Perpetual Peace that resulted in the marriage of Henry VII's daughter, Margaret, to James IV of Scotland. Wolsey presumably enjoyed this taste of foreign diplomacy, as, later in life, foreign affairs seem to have been his over-riding political interest.

On Deane's death in 1503, Wolsey became part of the household of Sir Richard Nanfan, Deputy Lieutenant of Calais. Peter Gwyn sees this as rather a come-down, but John Matusiak, Wolsey's most current biographer, in *"The Life of King Henry VIII's Cardinal"*, describes the opportunity quite differently.

Matusiak sees this as the period in Wolsey's career when he became thoroughly conversant with day-to-day administration of commercial, diplomatic and military affairs. Calais, the last English toe-hold in France, was the place where the majority of English exports were landed for transport into Europe. It was also a border town that had to be kept in a constant state of readiness, lest the French try to wrest it back.

The Deputy Lieutenant was answerable for everything that happened in Calais and its surrounding Pale. It was thus a position of great responsibility, and the elderly Nanfan entrusted much of the work to Wolsey. Wolsey probably spent the four years from 1503 to 1507 in Calais, returning to England on Nanfan's death.

Back in London, Wolsey obtained a post as Chaplain to the King himself. Henry VII's later years were overshadowed by gloom and a sense of repression – not altogether surprising when Henry's personal losses are considered. He lost a fifteen-month old son, a fifteen-year-old son, his wife and a new born baby all within the space of two years, as well as seeing his thirteen-year-old daughter depart for a new country. It would hardly be remarkable if he were depressed.

In true mediaeval fashion, the King, always religiously inclined, dealt with his sorrows by increasing his devotions, hearing several Masses daily and spending more time and money on his charitable projects. He would thus have had frequent contact with his Chaplains.

Wolsey is always seen as being Henry VIII's creation, but it is apparent that Henry VII recognised his talents almost immediately. Both Tudor kings were more than willing to promote men of ability, regardless of their background – partly because they recognised the importance of skill, and partly, no doubt to have servants who were dependent wholly on themselves for favour, without their own resources.

During this period, Wolsey also became close to Sir Thomas Lovell, and Richard Foxe, Bishop of Winchester, two of Henry VII's most trusted advisors. Lovell was President of the King's Council, Chancellor of the Exchequer (not the important role it is today, but not insignificant), Speaker of the House of Commons and Master of the King's Wards. Richard Foxe, although he had not been translated from his bishopric of Winchester to Canterbury on Deane's death, was Lord Privy Seal, and was closely involved in all matters of government, particularly foreign affairs. Wolsey became Foxe's Secretary and their relationship became one of personal trust and even affection, as evidenced by their letters in later times.

In 1508 Wolsey was sent by Henry VII to both Scotland, to negotiate over Border matters with James IV, and the Low Countries, on an embassy to the Emperor.

The trip to the Low Countries is one of the most famous episodes in Wolsey's early career. Apparently, he received the commission from the King at Richmond before noon, arrived in London by 4pm, took a barge to Gravesend and was there by 7pm, rode post to Dover, where he slept and took ship to Calais first thing in the morning, arriving by 10am. He then raced to the feet of the Emperor, whose court was not far across the border in Flanders, dispatched his business, returned to Calais that night, sailed in the morning, headed for London and was back at his post in Richmond early the next day. Henry, on seeing him, rebuked him for not having left, and was amazed to hear that Wolsey had been and returned.

The trip to Scotland was not quite so successful. James IV kept the delegation waiting in Berwick for five days. Even after he arrived, James was too busy to see him – he sent word that he was inspecting a gun-powder factory. Eventually, an audience was granted, and repeated over eight days. James, however, was not inclined to return the hostages that he was holding. Wolsey admitted to the King that there was some excuse for this as 'the offences of the Englishmen were to those of the Scotsmen as four to one'.

Wolsey was back in the Low Countries in the autumn of 1508, negotiating a second marriage for Henry VII with Marguerite of Austria, the Emperor's daughter, and Regent of the Low Countries. Nothing came of the negotiations but Wolsey was rewarded with the post of Almoner in

November 1508, and then, on 2nd February 1509, the position of Dean of Lincoln.

This was the last office that Henry VII granted Wolsey, as the King died on 21st April 1509. Wolsey was one of the clergy who followed the solemn procession behind Henry VII's coffin, as it was finally laid to rest in his new-built Chapel at Westminster Abbey on 8th May 1509.

Chapter 3: A New Reign (1509 – 1513)

There is some debate amongst historians as to whether Wolsey was passed over in the first few months of Henry VIII's reign, because of the dislike of that doyenne of the Tudor house, Lady Margaret Beaufort, Countess of Richmond and Derby, who was nominally regent for the remaining few weeks of Henry VIII's minority (he was not 18 until 28th June).

It is not clear whether Wolsey was not reappointed as Royal Chaplain, or whether he is just not mentioned in the various household lists. Biographers Williams and Matusiak contend the former, whilst Gwyn believes the latter. His post of Almoner initially went to Dr John Edenham, but Edenham died in September 1509 and Wolsey resumed the post.

Whether or not Wolsey was passed over in the spring and summer of 1509, he was certainly back in favour by the autumn and a string of offices came his way in the next four years: among others, Privy Councillor (by November 1509); Registrar of the Order of the Garter (April 1510); Prebend of St George, Windsor (February 1511) and Dean of York (February 1513).

So why was Wolsey so popular with the new king? There is, on this, as on so many things, two schools of thought. The first is that the young

Henry VIII had no interest in conducting government business, and wanted only to enjoy himself and spend his father's money. In this scenario, Henry is presented as easily led and strongly influenced by Wolsey, who was a witty and eloquent man. This idea is borne out by some of the later Ambassadors' reports about Wolsey really wielding the power, and Henry as a figurehead.

If one looks more closely, however, it is apparent from the internal government papers that Henry and Wolsey had a worked out what might nowadays be called a *'good cop-bad cop'* routine with one feigning anger or disgust at a foreign request whilst the other expressed regret that it couldn't be fulfilled and promised to look into it.

The other school of thought, is that Henry was always a clever man at choosing others to do the "grunt" work, but that he was always the ultimate arbiter, and that, as soon as Wolsey failed to deliver what the King wanted, he went.

It seems likely that in the early days of his reign, Henry, eighteen, handsome, gifted, athletic and energetic may have found the day-to-day details of administration dull and left them to his able Councillor, but, to quote Cavendish, he gave power to Wolsey because

'he was most earnest and readiest of all the King's Council to advance the King's only will and pleasure, without respect to the case.'

The King's Council, comprising about a dozen men, met regularly in the Star Chamber at Westminster. If Henry were not present, and it seems that during his early reign he was more frequently out hunting, then he needed a reliable go-between, and this seems to be the role that Wolsey took. It was not until the other Councillors found that this gave Wolsey a unique position of influence that they realised they had been side-lined.

Henry and Wolsey also got on well personally. Wolsey was described by the Venetian ambassador as *'handsome'* and even by his enemy Polydore Vergil (the historian of Henry VII's reign) as a man of distinction. He also had many tastes in common with Henry. He was musical (he played the lute and had a well-trained choir at a later date) was interested in building, and was a great patron of the Humanists.

Chapter 4: Wars & Alliances (1513 – 1515)

Wolsey really came to the fore in 1513. In that year, Henry embarked on a huge campaign in France, in alliance with his father-in-law, Ferdinand of Aragon, and the Holy Roman Emperor, Maximilian. A previous campaign in 1512, led by Wolsey's erstwhile pupil, Thomas Grey, now 2nd Marquess of Dorset, had ended in abject failure, blamed by Ferdinand on English incompetence.

Whilst there had been major problems with supplies, equipment and dysentery in the English army, part of the blame should lie with Ferdinand, who cared as much about Henry's claim to be King of France as he would have cared about a claim to be Emperor of China. He had used the English attack to divert the French, whilst scooping up his ultimate goal of the Kingdom of Navarre and then independently making peace with Louis XII.

In 1513, however, there was to a multi-pronged attack. Wolsey was in charge of the organisation of men and supplies. This was his chance to shine, and he took it, although he still consulted with Richard Foxe, Lord Privy Seal, and his earlier mentor.

The previous French campaign had been ill-armed, so thousands of suits of armour were ordered from Italy, heavy artillery was bought from Flanders and gun-powder was made in quantity and stored at the Tower of London, Southampton and Calais. At this point, Wolsey's previous knowledge of Calais must have proved enormously useful – the materiel was collected there in preparation for invasion. The pièces de resistance were twelve enormous cannon, known as the Twelve Apostles.

In anticipation of that later great general, Napoleon, Wolsey was aware that '*soldiers march on their stomachs*' and ordered the purchase and slaughter of 25,000 oxen (not forgetting to have money knocked off the deal for the return of the non-meat products). Even Englishmen could not march on beef alone, so malt, beans, oats and lamb were also procured.

Remembering that Ferdinand and Maximilian both had a long history of double-crossing their allies, Wolsey kept up a spy network to remain abreast of their doings, whilst still finding time to organise medical services for the troops, and most important of all, a constant supply of beer.

With such a finely provisioned army, there was no room for indiscipline, and Wolsey drew up the *Statutes of War* – a list of dos and don'ts for soldiers, including strict injunctions against robbery, sacrilege, molestation of civilians (in particular, no soldier was to enter a house where a woman was in childbed), arson and gambling. In an article that has a very modern resonance, soldiers were forbidden from making jibes about each other's place of origin.

The cost of all of this preparation was enormous, and further increased by the English agreement to pay 100,000 crowns to maintain Maximilian's army. Parliament had voted supplies, but there were murmurings when the tax collectors came to the door.

Whilst Henry and Wolsey were surpassing themselves in preparations for war, Ferdinand was surpassing himself in treachery, signing another secret deal with France. On the Anglo-Scottish border, too, pressure was mounting, as James IV, Henry's brother-in-law, declined to break off his alliance with France. James was in a difficult position, as he was in alliance with both countries, and at some point had to choose.

To deal with the Scottish threat, it was agreed, presumably by Henry, but with advice from Wolsey and Foxe, that Thomas Howard, Earl of Surrey, and his son, Lord Thomas Howard, would be left behind to repel any invasion from the north. It is apparent that the Howards wished to be involved in the main French campaign (another of Surrey's sons had been killed in a naval action off Brest, and they were keen for revenge).

It is perhaps from this banishment from the greatest force to head to France for a hundred years that the Howard antipathy to Wolsey can be dated – an antipathy that would play a significant part in his eventual downfall.

The campaign in France was successful, so far as it went. A couple of towns were captured, Therouanne and Tornai - the first territory won by an English army for sixty years. At the Battle of the Spurs the French cavalry were put to flight and some valuable prisoners, including the Duc de Longueville (1480-1516), were captured for ransom. Strategically, however, the towns were of far more benefit to Maximilian than they were to England, whilst the cost of the war had been huge.

Throughout the campaign, Wolsey had been busy organising, directing, planning and enabling his master to make a splendid show with brightly caparisoned horses, chests of treasure and silver plate. His closeness to the King can be gauged by the fact that Queen Katharine, left as Regent in England, wrote to Wolsey frequently, as well as to her husband. She even went so far as to ask Wolsey to ensure the King had dry shirts as she thought him susceptible to colds.

These wifely concerns were not the only thing on Katharine's mind. James IV had decided in favour of his old ally, France, and had invaded England. Surrey and his son, Lord Thomas Howard, were sent north whilst Katharine raised troops, got together what cash hadn't already been spent on the French adventure and headed north to meet her army. Before the Queen had passed Bedford, news of an overwhelming victory over the Scots king at Flodden reached her. James and a significant portion of his nobility had been killed.

Chapter 5: Diplomacy (1514 – 1518)

When Henry and Wolsey returned from France, it was to a seriously depleted treasury. Henry's ambition to emulate Henry V and conquer France could not realistically be supported.

A hundred years before, England had territory in France that it could use as a base, far larger than the Calais Pale and the new towns won. France itself had been riven with civil war and led by a king who suffered from severe mental disturbances. Things were very different by 1514. France was rich, united and led by a competent king, even though he was old by contemporary standards. The very idea that England, smaller, poorer and with a comparatively tiny population, could conquer France was a pipe-dream.

Henry may have wanted glory but he was not stupid, and he and Wolsey now looked to other means of making England a powerful force in Europe, which did not rely on war supported by unreliable allies. Both Maximilian and Ferdinand had taken Henry for a fool, and he would not forget the injury.

It had been agreed that Maximilian and Ferdinand's joint grand-son, Charles of Castile, would marry Henry's sister, Mary, on 15th May 1514, but Maximilian delayed and came up with excuses. His daughter, Marguerite, Regent of the Low Countries, urged her father to carry out the match as promised, but he continued to procrastinate.

Whether Henry and Wolsey had always intended to serve Maximilian a dose of his own medicine and double-cross him, or whether the preparations for Mary's wedding, which involved vast expense and complex preparation, were just a bluff, must remain unknown. Nevertheless, as soon as it was apparent that the wedding, (which would have made Mary of England Empress in due course), was off, Henry and Wolsey were ready with another plan.

England would ally with France, pleasing the new Pope, Leo X, who was considerably less bellicose than his predecessor, and driving a wedge between Maximilian to the north of France, and Ferdinand to the south.

The price was the marriage of Mary to Louis XII whose Queen, Anne of Brittany, had just died. Wolsey was a tough negotiator on the dowry and jointure, and Mary received some extraordinarily valuable jewels from her betrothed, who had no doubt heard her described as '*the most attractive woman ever seen.*' In addition, Henry was to be allowed to keep Tournai and receive the back payments of the pension due to the English Crown from France.

If Louis had lived long enough to give Mary a son, the English would have been cock-a-hoop. A regency presided over by the English King's sister would have been a splendid opportunity. As it was, Louis wore himself out undertaking his conjugal duties and was dead by New Year's Day 1515. During her marriage, Mary felt she was not well treated, and said to her brother that, had Wolsey accompanied her to France, rather than Norfolk, she would have been better handled.

The heir to the French throne, if Mary were not expecting a son, would be François d'Angouleme, married to Louis' daughter, Claude (French law did not permit the Crown to pass to a woman). Whilst Mary withdrew for the customary mourning period, François made strenuous efforts to seduce her, partly no doubt for personal pleasure, as he was a notorious womaniser, but partly to muddy any claim to the throne of a child she bore.

In the event, Mary was not pregnant, but she did cause a scandal by hastily marrying Charles Brandon, Duke of Suffolk, who had been sent to fetch her, after expressly swearing an oath in front of Wolsey and Henry that he would not entertain such a marriage.

The young couple, once they had realised the enormity of their actions, wrote to Wolsey, begging his intercession with the King, which Wolsey, after telling them what a dangerous situation they were in, promised. He intimated that hard cash would soften the King's anger considerably, and eventually they were forgiven on promise of paying a huge fine.

This personal intervention with the King at the request of Mary, who was a Dowager Queen and Henry's own sister, shows the extent of Wolsey's influence. It was now becoming the object of resentment by the King's nobles, and also by the Queen.

For the first five years of their marriage, Katharine was probably the single greatest influence on Henry, but she could never be completely happy with a French alliance, even though she had been horrified by her father's betrayal of her husband and had firmly sided with Henry. It is likely that she felt jealous at a personal level too. Most wives would resent being supplanted in their husband's confidence by a third party. Her dislike of Wolsey would only increase over the next ten years.

The treaty with France was renewed with François but the balance of power was about to shift dramatically again. François, much to Henry's chagrin, achieved a victory over the Emperor at Marignano in 1515 that was stunning in its magnitude, and assured François of the disputed Duchy of Milan.

France was now riding too high. Men were dispatched from England to offer large sums of money to the Emperor to pay Swiss mercenaries, whilst a show of amity with France continued. Simultaneously, overtures were made to Charles, Maximilian's grandson, now King of Spain. Maximilian wrote gleefully to Charles that Charles could dupe the English, whilst he duped the French. True to form, Maximilian took the English gold, raised an army, then failed to fight.

Another solution had to be thought of to keep the balance of power, and Wolsey came up with a plan that would, he hoped, satisfy everyone and redound to his credit for all ages to come. Pope Leo was preaching a crusade, and whilst that might sound as though it were an old fashioned concept by the sixteenth century, it should not be forgotten that the Turks were advancing on Hungary, which they were to conquer in 1526.

The plan was for all the Christian Princes of Europe to swear eternal brotherhood and then concentrate on defending Christendom. The Treaty of London was signed in 1518. Intended as a non-aggression pact, some twenty-five European states were involved. All were to come to the aid of any of their number, if attacked. Wolsey received much of the credit for the treaty:

'Undoubtedly, My Lord, God continuing it (the Treaty) shall be the best that ever was done for the realm of England and after the King's Highness the laud and praise shall be to you a perpetual memory.' – Bishop Foxe

Nevertheless, whilst the ink was still wet, most of the signatories were busy doing side deals. As part of a bilateral Anglo-French agreement, Henry VIII's daughter, Mary, was betrothed to the Dauphin.

Chapter 6: Archbishop & Cardinal

Late in 1514, Wolsey was promoted to the Archbishopric of York, second only to Canterbury in seniority, although a very distant second in terms of wealth and influence. William Warham, who had succeeded Wolsey's own master, Henry Deane, as Archbishop of Canterbury in 1503, showed no signs of dropping off his perch.

The receipt of the Archbishopric of York did not come without scandal. The previous incumbent, Cardinal Bainbridge, had spent much of his archiepiscopate as English Ambassador in Rome, and in July 1514 he died there. It was almost immediately discovered that he had been poisoned and eventually confirmed (by means of torture) that it had been at the hands of a servant of his rival, Silvestri, the Italian Bishop of Worcester, although Silvestri's involvement was never proven.

There were dark rumours that Wolsey had been concerned, although there was never any accusation or evidence brought, and, as Wolsey had stayed well away from the cesspit of politics that was the Roman Curia, it seems unlikely.

Wolsey then received the highest ecclesiastical office of all. After much badgering and even more bribing, Pope Leo X appointed him Cardinal on 10ᵗʰ September 1515. In due course, the red hat that Wolsey coveted so much was dispatched and treated with extraordinary ceremonial 'as though it were the greatest prince in Christendom come into the realm.' It was conveyed to London and placed on the High Altar at Westminster to be viewed reverently by the great and good of the realm.

A Mass was celebrated by Archbishop Warham, flanked by the Bishops of Armagh and Dublin. The sermon was preached by the Humanist John Colet, who observed, no doubt somewhat to Wolsey's chagrin, that his role was, like that of his ultimate master, Christ, to minister rather than being ministered to.

Leo refused, however, to give Wolsey the overriding power of *Legate a Latere* which would have given him overall control of English ecclesiastical matters. These were still in the hands of Warham.

This lack of jurisdiction was a disappointment to both Henry and Wolsey, as trouble was brewing between Church and State and, had Wolsey had a free hand, he would have bent the Church to Henry's will.

In 1512 Parliament had passed an Act limiting the right of Clergy to be tried only by Ecclesiastical Courts (the controversy that had raged in Henry II's time, resulting in the death of Thomas Becket). Not surprisingly, conservative churchmen were against this encroachment on the rights of the Church, and a conference was held at Blackfriars where Henry himself listened to arguments on both sides. In the end, he gave judgement, and, prefiguring a later controversy, announced:

'Kings of England in time past have never had any superior but God only...we will maintain the right of our crown and temporal jurisdiction...'

Archbishop Warham requested that the matter be adjudicated by Rome, but Henry did not grant this the dignity of an answer. Wolsey's exact position on the primacy of Church versus state cannot be stated with certainty, but it seems likely he agreed with Henry.

The 1510s were a period of increasing anti-clerical feeling, particularly in London, and this was compounded after 1517, by the spread of what the Church considered to be heresy. In previous ages the Church had responded to heresy by trying to persuade the heretic to abjure, or recant his heresies, in which case, he would be given a penance and brought back into the fold of the Church.

As the temperature on religious matters rose, and as more and more people began to espouse the new teachings, the Church took a more hard-line position. It is difficult for us to accept that burning people for their beliefs was considered the right response, but for the people of the time, a heretic was a dangerous criminal who could lead others into sin and imperil their souls. Tough measures were absolutely necessary to protect the innocent. The only variation was on the definition of heretic.

Wolsey, however, seems to have been disinclined to severe punishments for heretics. Whilst he was active in the searching out and burning of heretical works, primarily those coming in from Europe containing Lutheran ideas, he seems to have confined his punishments of heretics to either penance and forgiveness, or a whipping. Wolsey was, of course, for many, the embodiment of clerical sin. He was an absentee priest, he held numerous livings, he lived in a level of unimaginable luxury, and he was not as celibate as he ought to have been - he had a single, long-term relationship with Joan Larke, by whom he had two children.

Nevertheless, he seldom exerted himself to punish his severest critics. Even Robert Barnes (burnt in the 1530s, long after Wolsey's time, for heresy) who had written scathing attacks on the Cardinal, was admired for his skill in argument and encouraged to make a general submission in front of Wolsey rather than face the more stringent Episcopal court. Despite being well aware of the need for reform in Church matters and undertaking some mild improvements in his own Archdiocese, it was never a matter of urgency for Wolsey.

It has been claimed that Wolsey was desperate to be elected Pope, and he was put forward on two occasions – 1522 and 1523. Henry VIII pressed his candidacy and he was promised the support of the Emperor Charles, which extended as far as writing a letter that was deliberately delayed. However it is apparent from Wolsey's correspondence that he did not anticipate any likelihood of victory, and that he had no interest in being Pope. He made no effort to cultivate friends in Rome, never visited, and largely ignored the Roman politics surrounding Papal elections. It may be that in 1528 he regretted his failure to attend to his ecclesiastic career, but it was too late by then.

Where he did use his influence at Rome was to promote Henry VIII's book against Luther, *'Assertio Septem Sacramentorum'*. Wolsey wrote a dedication, and also made it very clear to Pope Leo that a suitable honorific would be a welcome gift to the King. Leo took the hint and bestowed the title of Defender of the Faith on Henry, which title has been proudly displayed on English, and British, coins ever since.

Chapter 7: Lord Chancellor

In 1514, Archbishop Warham resigned the Chancellorship in Wolsey's favour. Wolsey was not trained in either Civil or Canon Law and this was both a blessing and a curse in his role as Lord Chancellor. In those times the Lord Chancellor still acted as a judge, and it is apparent that Wolsey took this very seriously. Whilst he was gaining a terrible reputation for pride, arrogance and avarice, he was also winning plaudits as a man who dispensed swift, impartial justice.

'He has the reputation of being extremely just; he favours the people exceedingly, and especially the poor, hearing their suits and seeking to dispatch them instantly.' – Venetian Ambassador

He was not interested in the niceties of the law, and would move suits from Common Law courts to Chancery which inevitably drew the enmity of Common Law lawyers, but it gave the principle of Equity in law a new lease of life. It soon became obvious that he would not tolerate law breaking by even the highest in the land. Nobles and gentlemen who were used to having their own way in the local Assize Courts were swiftly disabused of their belief that they were above the law. This may sound admirable to us, but it made Wolsey no friends at the time.

This lack of deference to his 'betters', and the ostentation and magnificence of his general demeanour (his Cardinal's hat was treated as though it were a holy relic), was creating a huge groundswell of resentment amongst the other men who surrounded the King.

A fine example of this is the imprisonment in the Fleet prison of no less a personage than the Earl of Northumberland for retaining ie having men at arms in his pay, wearing his livery instead of the King's. Another aspect of Wolsey's impartial law enforcement that earned him many enemies at court, was the rigorous enforcement of the laws against enclosure of land that had been passed by Parliament in 1517-18, but were frequently ignored by high-ranking men.

Chapter 8: Arbiter of Europe (1518 – 1522)

Not long after the Treaty of London was signed, Emperor Maximilian died, upsetting the balance of power again. The most likely successor was Charles of Castile, but, as the office of Emperor was elected, not inherited, other men could put their name forward, and François I immediately did so.

Henry VIII was also, for a time, mesmerised by the thought of an Imperial crown, but despite some mild efforts and sweeteners by England and some enormous bribes from François, Charles emerged, at the age of 19, as the secular leader of Christendom. Wolsey seems to have been half-hearted in supporting Henry's claims, no doubt aware that Charles' election was a racing certainty.

The election of Charles V meant that the power previously divided between the Empire and Spain was now concentrated in a single man. To countervail this, relations with France needed to be improved again. It was agreed that Henry and François would meet, and both Kings gave Wolsey the task of organising what turned out to be one of the costliest (and most pointless) junkets in history, the Field of Cloth of Gold. Taking place in June of 1520 at the Val d'Or, near Calais, it was an opportunity for Henry and François to meet, and hopefully, forge a personal bond.

Wolsey was, perhaps, naïve, or had forgotten his own youth. There was never any possibility that two young men (30 and 26 years old) both bursting with testosterone and each keen to prove himself as the most chivalrous, brave and successful king in Europe, would ever be anything but rivals. The two Queens, Katharine and Claude, seem to have got on well, but Henry and François, despite Wolsey's best efforts to keep them from direct rivalry, insisted on an endless game of one-up-man-ship.

Even before the meeting, France was aggrieved because Henry had received a visit from the Emperor Charles in May 1520. François assumed, not without reason, that they were plotting against him. His fears were further exacerbated when Henry and Katharine left, not to return home as anticipated, but to cross the border into Flanders to meet Charles and his aunt, Regent Marguerite, at Gravelines.

Although Katharine's influence with Henry had waned by 1520, they were still on good terms, and Katharine was always going to favour an alliance with her nephew. To be fair to Henry and Wolsey, they resisted Charles' immediate blandishments and did not enter into his latest scheme against France at this time.

As François and Charles moved inevitably towards war again (Charles could not stomach France's supremacy in Milan), Wolsey offered himself as arbiter. Whilst Wolsey had many faults, it seems unfair not to accept that he was a man more inclined to peace and compromise than war and waste. His own self-satisfaction (the son of a butcher to play mediator to an Emperor) was no doubt was one of his motives, but a true desire for stability and peace in Europe was there as well.

In Wolsey's own words mediation avoided war and '*the consuming of treasure, subversion of realms, depopulation and desolation of countries*'. Only if arbitration failed would England support the country attacked, in accordance with the Treaty of London.

Wolsey journeyed to Calais in 1521 to attempt to reconcile François and Charles. Charles refused to attend negotiations at Calais, and would only receive Wolsey if he went to the Emperor at Bruges. His biographers differ on his motivations for events that occurred. Neville Williams, in "*The Cardinal and the Secretary*", takes this at face value, and believes that Wolsey's summons by Charles was genuine. Matusiak, on the other hand, suggests that this was a ruse to allow Wolsey to meet with Charles away from the French delegation and negotiate a separate treaty. It was undoubtedly Henry's policy to form an alliance with Charles, but whether Wolsey was deliberately disingenuous at Calais is debatable.

Regardless of Wolsey's inner feelings, an Anglo-Imperial treaty was signed that stipulated that, should France and the Empire fail to make peace by May 1522, England would send an army in support of Charles. The betrothal between Henry's five year old daughter, Mary, and François' son was to be broken off, and she was to marry Charles, when she reached the age of 12.

Once the agreement with England was made, Charles showed himself utterly intransigent on the negotiations with France.

'The more towardly disposition I find in the French party, the more sticking and difficulty be found in (Charles' delegates)' 'Wolsey wrote in despair.

Whilst acting in his capacity as arbiter, Wolsey surpassed himself with display – dressed in red taffeta, attended by scores of men and surrounded with the costliest plate and jewels. Any glory accorded to his minister reflected well on Henry and this is one of the reasons given by Wolsey for his excessive pomp and magnificence.

He did not seem to understand that embracing the Emperor or the King of France from his mule, as was the prerogative of fellow-monarchs, was not likely to endear him either to them, or to Henry's nobles who would not have dreamed of taking such liberties.

Chapter 9: Difficult Times (1522 – 1525)

The failure of the peace talks at Calais, whether or not Wolsey had been sincere, and the Treaty of Bruges made with Charles, meant that England was now, once more, committed to war to the tune of 40,000 men and horse, plus a fleet. Henry was delighted with Wolsey, sending letters in which he

'thanked God [he had] such a chaplain by whose wisdom fidelity and labour [he] could obtain greater acquisitions than all [his] progenitors were able to accomplish with all their numerous wars and battles.'

The talks with Charles were followed up by a state visit by the Emperor, which, again, Wolsey was responsible for arranging. Whilst not on the scale of the Field of Cloth of Gold, it was still impressive. It was agreed between the monarchs that any disagreement would be arbitrated by Wolsey. Charles must have been grinding his teeth, but the prospect of obtaining England through marriage, and achieving his ancestors' goal of completely encircling France, presumably made it worth his while to accept the dominance of Henry's cardinal.

Henry might have been excited at the prospect of renewed war, but Parliament was not. There was no alternative to calling Parliament – the anticipated costs of the campaign were nearly £400,000. A Commission had been sent out in March 1522 to assess the taxable worth of land, houses and valuables, and the City of London had been 'persuaded' to offer a loan of £20,000, but this was nowhere near adequate.

Parliament was called in April 1523. Wolsey, as Lord Chancellor, explained Henry's need for money, emphasising the treachery of the old enemy, France. He then asked for the unbelievable sum of £800,000, equivalent to a 20% tax across the board.

The Speaker of the Commons, Sir Thomas More, urged obedience to the King, but the Commons could not accept the demand. They asked Wolsey to request the King to take less, but Wolsey treated them roughly and refused to countenance such an idea. He then went to Parliament in his full glory, robed in red, with his Cardinal's hat and his Lord Chancellor's Seal, to intimidate the Commons. The House sat in silence, neither refusing, agreeing nor debating. Eventually, humiliated, the Cardinal left.

At last, a subsidy of 10% was voted, but there were murmurings across the country. Wolsey augmented the grant with a massive levy of 50% of a year's income on the Church, which he forced through as Legate, overriding Warham.

Despite the pain involved in raising the funds, the campaign of 1522-23 was a shambles. Unlike in 1513 when the English army had been considered a model of good behaviour, the campaign was largely about desecrating and laying waste the French countryside. Eventually, bogged down by the rain and mud of northern France, as every army in European history has been, the commander, the Earl of Surrey, withdrew to Calais, to await a further advance in 1523 under the Duke of Suffolk.

Suffolk too, after initial promising gains, failed to make any serious progress. The appalling conditions *'which caused the soldiers daily to die'* led him to advocate a retreat, but Henry was adamant. Wolsey had interfered in military matters and should have borne some of the responsibility for the fiasco, but Henry appears to have heaped all the blame on Suffolk. Suffolk may have owed Wolsey a favour for helping him when in disgrace over his marriage, but this reverse wiped out all gratitude and pushed Suffolk firmly into the growing camp of Wolsey's enemies.

By 1524, the failure of Charles to keep his side of the bargain, and the exhortations of the new Pope, Clement VII, for peace, inclined England to begin making overtures towards France again. François was not particularly interested in coming to terms – his sights were firmly on Italy. He crossed the Alps, heading for his Duchy of Milan, secured nine years earlier at Marignano. This time, however, it was the Emperor's turn for glory. On Charles V's birthday, 24th February 1525, the Spanish-Imperial army won a crushing victory at Pavia, taking François prisoner and annihilating his army.

Back in England, Henry was initially delighted, jumping out of bed to run to his wife and share the good news. Now would be the time for Charles and him to dismember France. Soon enough, though, it became apparent that Charles had no more interest in helping Henry to the French Crown than his grandfathers, Ferdinand and Maximilian, had had. Moreover, he no longer needed the English alliance to be cemented by his marriage to Henry's daughter.

Henry, still keen to press the advantage of a France in turmoil, proposed to lead yet another invasion. The question was how to fund it.

There was no hope of Parliament voting another subsidy, so Wolsey hit on the idea of a loan, the *'Amicable Grant'*, based on the feudal prerogative of the King being *'aided'* with money if he led an army abroad in person. The idea was no doubt taken up with glee by the King and Council, but the result was a miserable failure. Despite bullying in person by Wolsey, London refused to cough up. In the provinces, the Commissioners sent to collect it (including Sir Thomas Boleyn) were manhandled. East Anglia was close to open rebellion.

Henry, seriously worried, cancelled the grant. He was not pleased with Wolsey. Not pleased at all.

Troubles came thick and fast as the Emperor came to terms with France, and, in the Treaty of Madrid, allowed François to return home, with a new wife (Charles' sister) but minus a huge sum of cash, and his two sons, who were sent to Spain as sureties. Charles also calmly announced that he would not be marrying Princess Mary after all, but would seek a bride from wealthy Portugal. The rest of Europe was now horrified at Charles' overwhelming strength, and united in the Treaty of The More, negotiated again by Wolsey and signed on 30th August 1525 at his home.

Chapter 10: The King's Secret Matter (1525 – 1529)

By 1525, Wolsey's only friend was the King. The nobles hated and were envious of him; Queen Katharine believed he was favouring the French over her Spanish connection; the Church at home resented his financial exactions, and the Pope was not impressed by his lack of interest in keeping Rome informed of events. Emperor Charles and King François had been thoroughly offended by his pride, and the only person to have a good word for him was Charles' aunt, Marguerite, Regent of the Low Countries, whose power was limited.

But these were all known enemies – Wolsey had also crossed someone who would be far more dangerous to him than all the rest put together – Anne Boleyn.

Cavendish's *"Life of Cardinal Wolsey"* is the source for the story that Wolsey had incurred Anne's enmity in the early 1520s by breaking off her romance with Henry Percy, heir to the Earl of Northumberland. According to Cavendish, this had been instigated by the King himself, but Anne vowed revenge on the Cardinal. If she did, he no doubt dismissed it as angry talk by a mere girl. If the Queen could not influence her husband against him, what chance did Anne have?

However, by 1525, Henry VIII had fallen in love with Anne, and, before long, was planning to marry her. It would do a real disservice to Henry to believe that infatuation with Anne was his only reason for seeking an annulment of his marriage. Katharine had not had a pregnancy for seven years, and it seemed her child-bearing days were done. Henry thus had no legitimate male heir, and there were concerns about female succession. In addition, the betrayal of England by Charles and his rejection of Princess Mary meant that the Anglo-Spanish alliance that Katharine represented was now outworn.

Whether Anne was a suitable choice for a second match is a different matter, and, probably, at the start of the annulment proceedings, not a definite decision.

Wolsey was blamed then, and subsequently, for Henry's decision to seek an annulment, however, Henry himself stated that Wolsey had, instead, tried to dissuade him. Wolsey was all too aware of the difficulties that would need to be overcome for Henry to gain his freedom. First, the Pope would have to admit that his predecessor had been wrong to grant a dispensation for the marriage, and, second, the

Emperor would have to accept the Pope's decision and see his aunt and cousin humiliated.

In May 1527 Henry's campaign opened when Wolsey constituted a secret court, presided over by himself and Archbishop Warham, that cited Henry to appear to answer a charge of living in sin with his brother's widow. Henry therefore was a defendant, and appointed a proxy to act for him, brandishing the dispensation granted by Pope Julius II in 1503.

It was open to Wolsey and Warham to state that the dispensation was insufficient, and perhaps, had they done so, the matter might have passed quickly into the realms of the *fait accompli*. However, they could not bring themselves to take the hazardous and potentially sinful step of ruling that a Papal dispensation was invalid. They therefore ruled that the matter was open to doubt, and would have to be adjudicated in Rome.

Henry was not, of course, the first king or noble to seek an annulment, and generally, matters proceeded fairly smoothly. Some technical fault was found and the deed was done, with general face-saving all round. In some cases the discarded wives (it was usually, but not always, a wife who was discarded) were persuaded to enter a convent, which allowed the husband to remarry.

In the mid-1520s however, the situation was clouded by two factors – first, the spread of Lutheran ideas challenging the supremacy of the Pope. Clement VII would not be eager to add fuel to these notions by suggesting his predecessor had been wrong to grant the dispensation under which Henry and Katharine were originally married. The second obstacle was the sack of Rome by Emperor Charles' forces in May 1527, which resulted in the Pope becoming his prisoner.

Wolsey tried to turn this situation to advantage, by travelling to Avignon, France, in a bid to be recognised as the Pope's regent, able to act for him whilst he was in bondage. However, he was circumvented, first by Katharine smuggling a letter out to Charles V, and by the immediate efforts of his enemies at home to undermine him as soon as he was out of the country. The King was persuaded by Anne's faction, which combined Anne's relatives with Wolsey's enemies (her uncle, the Duke of Norfolk, her father, Sir Thomas Boleyn and Charles Brandon, Duke of Suffolk being the ringleaders) to send messengers directly to Rome.

Wolsey failed in his trip to Avignon, the other Cardinals not showing any enthusiasm for Wolsey as the Pope's deputy, and returned to England in September 1527. Henry's messengers had met with no more success than Wolsey's move, so Wolsey was once more expected to come up with a solution. He persuaded Clement to grant a commission to Wolsey, and a fellow Cardinal, Lorenzo Campeggio (who was also Bishop of Salisbury) to hear the case and pronounce on it. Whilst Clement would not openly agree to accept the verdict, he gave a private letter, assuring them he would, whilst, at the same time telling Campeggio the letter was not to be used, and could only be shown to Henry and Wolsey.

In 1529, the famous Legatine Court opened at Blackfriars to try the case of matrimony between Henry VIII and Katharine of Aragon. After some opening legal business, Katharine famously appealed to her husband in person, then refused to accept the authority of the Court, appealing directly to Rome. Clement was horrified, but unable to resist the pressure of the Emperor, who now controlled Italy, removed the authority of the Blackfriars Court. On 31st July 1529 Wolsey was obliged to stand up in Court and tell the King that his case was not concluded, but must be heard in Rome.

Chapter 11: The End (1529 – 1530)

Henry had suspected for some time, owing to the seeds of doubt planted by Anne and her supporters, that Wolsey was not as diligent in pursuing the annulment as Henry required, and the failure of the Legatine Court seemed to support that fear. He was not, however, certain that he could, or should, try to manage without Wolsey. He also remained personally attached to the Cardinal.

Wolsey was in disgrace, but Campeggio asked that he be permitted to accompany him on Campeggio's visit to Grafton in Northamptonshire to take his leave of Henry. Henry agreed, much to the chagrin of Anne. When Wolsey arrived, it was to find there was no room for him at the house, but Sir Henry Norris, one of the King's gentlemen, took pity on him and let him use his own room.

On being allowed into the King's presence, the Cardinal was unusually deferential to his assembled enemies, but he was soon chatting familiarly to the King again, tucked in a window embrasure, exchanging confidences.

Overnight, however, Anne hatched a plan to take the King hunting on the following day, leaving Wolsey to accompany Campeggio back to London. The knives were now out for Wolsey. He was indicted for *'praemunire'* (the useful expedient that was brought out from time to time to keep the Church in its place and which consisted of a charge of putting the Church above the King), which he admitted, beseeching the King to forgive him.

'I, your poor, heavy and wretched priest do daily pursue, cry and call upon Your Royal Majesty for grace, mercy, remission and pardon...'

In October 1529, Wolsey was stripped of his position of Lord Chancellor and told to remove from York House to Esher. En route, he was met by Sir Henry Norris, with a ring from the King. Grateful beyond words, Wolsey sank to his knees in the road, thanking the King for his kindness, which he reciprocated by sending his fool, Patch to the King's service – much to Patch's displeasure - he had to be taken by force.

Henry again sent positive messages in November, before Parliament opened, but Wolsey's enemies were baying for his blood, and the Lords introduced a bill to prevent Henry ever employing him in public office again. The bill contained an enormous list of, mainly ludicrous, charges, including embezzlement, putting the Cardinal's hat on the coinage, referring to himself in the same sentence as the King, and endangering the King's health by breathing infection on him. Wolsey was ably defended in the Commons by his secretary, Thomas Cromwell, and the bill was dropped. The King, meanwhile, agreed to make such provision as he thought fit, bearing in mind the articles in the original bill. He did not wish to commit himself to never employing Wolsey again.

In the new year of 1530, Norfolk continued his assault, but, when Wolsey fell seriously ill, Henry exclaimed that he would not lose him for £20,000 and sent his own doctors, as well as another ring. He also persuaded Anne to send a token of esteem. Nevertheless, the pressure from Norfolk, Suffolk, Boleyn and the rest was unrelenting – it was now a fight to the death. If Henry re-established Wolsey in his favour, they could not hope to survive.

The Council, unable to persuade Henry to completely abandon him, went along with a full pardon on 12th February, together with banishment to reside in his Archbishopric of York. Wolsey pleaded poverty and attempted to persuade the French and Imperial courts to send the arrears of pensions promised many years before. Henry, too, sent him £1,000. In April, he began his journey north. He remained at the Archbishopric's house at Southwell for some months, living more ostentatiously than was wise, in direct contravention of Cromwell's advice.

Wolsey, who had been so aware of the shifts of power, and had used his knowledge of men to attain the heights he had, now seemed to lose his head completely. He had obviously not grasped the level of Henry's attachment to Anne Boleyn, and he sought to undermine Norfolk, and the process of the annulment by writing to the Imperial Ambassador and taking an interest in Katharine's case.

Always busy, Wolsey occupied his time in his diocese acting more in conformity with his vows as a priest than ever before – dispensing charity, Confirming children and saying Mass. He had never actually been enthroned as Archbishop, so, despite needing the King's consent, which he neglected to ask for, he sent out summons to the northern convocation of clergy to attend his enthronement on 7th November 1530.

This, together with information that a Papal Bull, threatening excommunication had been published, was enough to allow Henry to be persuaded that Wolsey was guilty of *'presumptuous, sinister practices'*. On 1st November, a warrant was issued for his arrest. On 4th November Wolsey was arrested and carried towards London. By Saturday, 26th November, he was at the Greyfriars Abbey, Leicester. He had been sickening all the while, and, tumbling from his mule, told the Abbot that he was *'come hither to leave (his) bones amongst (them)'*.

He died on the following Tuesday, uttering the famous words:

'If I had served my God as diligently as I have served my King, He would not have given me over in my grey hairs.'

He was buried in the Abbey church, close to the grave of Richard III.

Wolsey was, without doubt, one of the proudest, vainest and most arrogant men to wield power in England, yet he was also devoted to his king, a promoter of peace where that was practicable, and determined to give England an important place in foreign affairs. He was a patron of the arts and of education, and upheld the law impartially against the rich as well as the poor, whilst avoiding the harsh religious punishments so popular with his contemporaries. He worked indefatigably for the advancement of his country, and deserves a better reputation than he has.

Aspects of Cardinal Wolsey's Life

Chapter 12: Patron of Education

Wolsey was nothing if not grand in his vision. As a man who had risen high in the world, through his education, he determined to emulate some of his great ecclesiastical predecessors, such as William Wykeham, Bishop of Winchester, founder of Wolsey's own alma mater, Magdalen College, Oxford and found both a school and university college.

The college came first, with preparations beginning in 1524, and then the school in 1528. Even Wolsey's wealth was not sufficient for his ambitions, so he planned to fund the building work and endow the colleges through the suppression of some smaller monasteries, and the diversion of their wealth.

Cardinal College, Oxford – now Christ Church

The site chosen was the Augustinian St Frideswide's Priory and a Bull was received in 1524 from Pope Clement VII, permitting its suppression. The site was extended to include surrounding houses, the Oxford Jewish quarter, various inns and also Canterbury College.

Works began almost immediately, with the centrepiece being the Gothic quadrangle known as *'Tom Quad'* which, measuring 264 by 261 feet, is still the largest in Oxford. By the time of Wolsey's fall in 1529, the building work was incomplete, with only three sides of the quadrangle finished, and the fourth, the Chapel location, still at foundation level. The Hall was finished, worked on by the mason Thomas Redman and the glazier James Nicholson, as were the kitchens.

The College was to be staffed by a Dean (the first being John Higdon, formerly a Fellow at Magdalen with Wolsey) and sixty Canons, as well as a schoolmaster, priests, clerks and choir boys, honest paupers (!) and undergraduates.

Work stopped in 1529, then, in 1532, Cardinal College was re-founded as King Henry VIII's College, on a reduced scale, with only twelve canons.

On 20th May 1545, the College was surrendered to the Crown, as one of the last monasteries in England, and combined with the see of Oxford to create the new Christ Church, Oxford, which remains the Cathedral Church of the Diocese of Oxford.

Cardinal College, Ipswich

The plan was for a college of secular canons – that is, ordained priests who live in community as monks do, but go into the world to practise their ministry – together with a school for boys to act as a feeder for Cardinal College at Oxford.

The site selected was originally the priory of St Peter and St Paul, but Wolsey received a Bull from Pope Clement VII on 28th May, 1528 allowing the suppression of the monastery, confirmed by Henry VIII. In addition to the closure of St Peter and Paul (whose inmates were to be moved to other priories of the same order), a further ten monasteries (Snape, Dodnash, Wikes, Tiptree, Horkesley, Rumburgh, Felixstowe, Bromhill, Blythburgh, and Mountjoy) were also closed, and the land and funds diverted to the new College. Funds from the Church of St Nicholas, where Wolsey's father had been a Church Warden, and also from St. Peter, St.-Mary-at-Quay, St. Clement, and St. Matthew were diverted to the College.

The foundation stone was laid on 20th June 1528 by John Longland, Bishop of Lincoln, another ex-colleague of Wolsey's at Magdalen, and a couple of weeks later the formal royal licence for the Cardinal's College of St Mary, Ipswich, was granted by the King at Hampton Court.

The licence gave details of how the College would be manned. There were to be a Dean, twelve priests, eight clerks, eight singing boys and poor scholars, and thirteen poor men. Their role was to pray for the health and well-being of the King and the Cardinal, and for the souls of the Cardinal's parents. There was also to be one schoolmaster, learned in (Latin) grammar to teach the scholars and any others who came to the college, from any part of the country. The first Dean was Dr William Capon, Master of Jesus College, Cambridge and the school master was William Goldwin. The College was to be free from the normal supervision of the local Bishop.

As well as the organisation of the religious side, Wolsey took a keen personal interest in the scholars. He selected the Latin grammar book that was to be used, and wrote a special preface for it – rather pompous in tone, but his motives were good, and he was clear that competent school masters were necessary. The instructions for the school cast a light on an under-appreciated, but attractive aspect of Wolsey's character – his fundamental dislike of physical punishment. In an age that believed that to '*spare the rod was to spoil the child*', he wrote

'We admonish particularly, that tender youth be not effected by severe stripes or threatening countenance or by any species of tyranny.'

He also enjoined the parents of his boys to send them to Ipswich with sufficient warm clothes for chilly East Anglian winters.

A great inaugural dinner was held in early September 1528, for which Anne Howard, Countess of Oxford sent two fine bucks, and her brother, the Duke of Norfolk, other supplies. At the same time, vast quantities of plate and vestments were brought by Wolsey's staff, including Thomas

Cromwell and Rowland Lee. Cromwell apparently took 'great pains' to arrange everything.

On 7th September, there was a solemn procession in St Peter's Church (which was to continue as the College Church) for the service of Evensong. This was followed by a procession to the Lady Chapel, where Evensong was performed again. The following day, the planned procession, at which the Dean, Subdean, six priests, eight clerks, nine choristers, and all their servants who had attended on 7th, were to be joined by the Bailiffs and dignitaries of the town, was cancelled, owing to incessant rain.

A damp service was held in Holy Trinity, with the Bishop of Norwich in attendance. Dean Capon was pleased with the singers, but they complained that they had received better wages in their previous positions. There were also the usual complaints that everyone had too much to do, and that more staff were needed, as the five priests already in post were not enough to keep three Masses a day. The Sub-dean, Mr Ellis, was too busy to take a hand as he was managing the building works.

The choir master, Mr Lentall, took to his work with delight, promising 'there shall be no better children in any place in England than we shall have here shortly.'

Building works began with 120 tons of white Caen stone being delivered in early September 1528, with a further 100 to arrive by Michaelmas (29th September) and a thousand to be supplied before Easter 1529. Works continued apace in 1529, and on 24th July Cromwell received a letter informing him that the works were now above the ground and that the site was busy night and day.

Wolsey fell from power before the College was finished. On 14th November 1530 Commissioners arrived from the King to value everything on site. All the plate and valuables were seized, and Dr Capon accused of hiding £1,000 worth of goods. On 21st November, the Duke of

Norfolk's men took possession of the site and in 1531, the site of the College, and its Ipswich possessions were granted to Thomas Alvard, one of Henry's gentleman ushers. Some of the other property was granted to Eton College and some to the Abbey of Waltham. The site itself fell into disrepair and was used as a rubbish dump.

Chapter 13: Following the Footsteps of Thomas Wolsey

Wolsey travelled largely in the south-east of England, with a number of visits to Calais, the Low Countries, France, and Scotland during his life. The numbers in brackets refer to the key to the map below.

Born in Ipswich (1), he first left it in around 1485 to travel to Oxford where he studied at Magdalen College (2) and later founded Cardinal's College (now Christ Church College). Whilst acting as schoolmaster to the sons of the Marquess of Dorset, he went with the young men to their home at Bradgate, Leicestershire (3). This is likely to have been his first taste of the delights of wealth. His first modest living, however, as a priest, was at St Mary's Limington (4), Somerset, although whether he ever actually lived there is a moot point.

He was certainly back in London by 1501, in residence at Lambeth Palace (5). His next port of call was a stint in Calais, as assistant to the Deputy Lieutenant, Sir Richard Nanfan. On returning home in 1507, he joined the royal household, which was mainly centred on Henry VII's new palace at Richmond (6). Whilst in Henry's employ, he visited both Scotland and the Low Countries on diplomatic missions.

Wolsey's first great step forward in the Church was his preferment as Dean, then Bishop of Lincoln (7), although, if he went to the cathedral at all, it would have been a fleeting visit. He certainly did not take up residence.

Promoted to the Archbishopric of York in 1514, Wolsey took possession of York Place (8), the Archbishops' palace in London, which is now the location of Whitehall. York Place had been largely ignored by the previous incumbent, Cardinal Bainbridge, and Wolsey set about renovating the palace on a grand scale. The chief architect was Henry Redmayne, who was the master mason of Westminster Abbey. Overall, the renovations cost in excess of £1,250 in a time when a soldier earned 4d a day.

But York Place belonged to the Church – Wolsey wanted a place of his own. In 1514 he acquired Hampton Court (9), which he transformed into the most glittering renaissance palace in Britain, outstripping Henry VII's great construction at Richmond, and the King's favourite palace at Greenwich. Henry looked on Hampton Court with covetous eyes, and, in 1528, when times were becoming difficult for Wolsey, he gave it to the King, although with the proviso that he could stay there whenever he liked.

Not content with Hampton Court, Wolsey also acquired and spent considerable amounts of time during the 1520s at The More (10), near Rickmansworth. After his fall, this was the house to which Katharine of Aragon was banished.

During the period 1520 – 22, Wolsey travelled to Calais, in charge of the preparations for the Field of Cloth of Gold, and then for the negotiations of 1522, first in Calais, then in Bruges. In 1527 he was abroad again, heading for Avignon in the south of France, to persuade the College of Cardinals to accept him as deputy for the imprisoned pope, Clement VII.

One of the most significant scenes of Wolsey's life was played out at Blackfriars (11) – this was a Dominican monastery, but was frequently used for Parliament meetings or for other state occasions. It is now buried beneath Blackfriars station. In May 1529, Blackfriars was the location of the Legatine Court presided over by Wolsey and Cardinal Campeggio, to try the matrimonial cause between Henry VIII and Katharine of Aragon.

Wolsey's failure to obtain the annulment led to his fall from favour. He was given hope of reinstatement in Henry's good graces when he was graciously received by the King at Grafton Regis (12), but he was disappointed.

Sent to reside in his diocese of York, Wolsey took up residence, first at Southwell in Nottinghamshire, then at the Archbishops' Palace at Cawood Castle (13). Here too, he could not resist his desire to build and improve, and began spending money on renovations. Here too, he planned his enthronement at York Minster (14), but he was arrested, and died at Greyfriars Abbey, Leicester (15) before it could take place.

The most interesting thing about Wolsey's journeys, is not the actual locations, but the ceremony and pageantry that followed him as he went. Wherever he was, Wolsey would make the most of his appearance to strike awe and wonder into the watching crowds. As became a Prince of the Church, he rode a mule, but the mule would be trapped with gold, and his retinue in red satin.

Whilst he was residing at York Place in the period after 1514, he would visit the King at Greenwich each Sunday. Setting out early in the morning, he would descend the new water steps he had had built, into his painted and gilded barge, attended by a liveried retinue. He would be rowed downstream as far as either Queenhithe (now Cannon Street) or St Paul's.

Once arrived, he would leave the barge and be met by horses which would carry him past the treacherous rapids at London Bridge, then some 100 ft (30 meters) further downstream than now. 'Shooting the bridge', as it was called, when a vessel passed downstream under it, was a dangerous undertaking and avoided if at all possible. Past London Bridge, he would enter another barge to continue to Greenwich.

All the other days of the week, when he was in London, Wolsey would travel to Westminster to undertake his duties in the Star Chamber and in Chancery. Leaving York Place at 8am he would be preceded by two great silver crosses, one each for his roles as Papal Legate and Archbishop. These would be followed by two pillars of state, the Lord Chancellor's Sergeant-at-arms and a page, bearing the Great Seal in a silk bag. Wolsey would come next on his mule, his four footmen bearing silver poleaxes and a peer or a gentleman usher bearing his red cardinal's hat. To clear the crowds, ushers marched ahead, crying 'On, my Lords and Masters. Make way for my Lord's Grace, The Cardinal Legate of York, Lord High Chancellor of this realm.'

The most magnificent trip of all was Wolsey's foray toward the French camp at the Field of Cloth of Gold, when he left the English camp to arrange the details of the two Kings' meeting.

He set forth on his mule, with fifty mounted gentlemen preceding him, gowned in red velvet and a further fifty ushers bearing gold maces as 'large as a man's head'. In front of him was borne his great gold cross, with a jewelled crucifix. Behind the Cardinal rode a phalanx of bishops and other clergy, including the Grand Prior of the Knights of St John of Jerusalem. Bringing up the rear, were 100 mounted archers of the King's Guard.

It is not hard to see why Henry's nobles considered Wolsey an arrogant upstart.

Key to Map

1. Ipswich
2. Magdalen and Christ Church, Oxford
3. Bradgate Park, Leicestershire

4. St Mary's Church, Limington, Somerset

5. Lambeth Palace, London

6. Richmond Palace, London

7. Lincoln Cathedral

8. York Place, London

9. Hampton Court Palace, Surrey

10. The More, near Rickmansworth, Hertfordshire

11. Blackfriars Monastery, London

12. Grafton Regis , Northamptonshire

13. Cawood Castle near Selby, Yorkshire

14. York Minster, Yorkshire

15. Church of the Greyfriars, Leicester

Ruins

No trace

In Current Use

Later Replaced

Chapter 14: Thomas Wolsey: In History & Literature

History

Wolsey was one of the first politicians and statesmen in England to be the subject of a biography. His early biographer was George Cavendish (brother of the Sir William Cavendish whose descendants are now Dukes of Devonshire). Cavendish was Wolsey's Gentleman-Usher in the last few years of his life. Thus, he was not only close to Wolsey in his triumph, but his position gave him access when Wolsey had less to do, and was therefore more inclined to talk to his attendants at length about the past.

Cavendish's biography, which is still in print, is a very positive portrait of his master.

Far less complimentary were Polydore Vergil and Edward Hall. Vergil, who is generally a balanced reporter, had a personal grudge against Wolsey, whom he believed had blocked him from promotion, and Edward Hall was a reformer who saw Wolsey as the exemplification of every ill of the old Church.

Throughout the following centuries Wolsey was seen as a villain – an early attempt by Richard Fiddes in 1724 to rescue his reputation was roundly condemned for casting aspersions on the glory of the Reformation. It was not until the late nineteenth century that he was rehabilitated by historians such as Creighton, who saw in his efforts to make England centre stage in European politics a foreshadowing of Empire.

In the twentieth century he was the subject of a major biography in the 1920s by that colossus of Tudor History, A F Pollard. Pollard is definitely of the school that believes Wolsey wanted to be Pope, and that he dominated Henry VIII.

Much of Pollard's basic thesis is overturned by Dr Peter Gwyn, in which several hundred pages of densely printed text give a complete picture of the political ins and outs in England between the years 1509 and 1530. Gwyn convincingly shows that Henry was in charge all along, but, the work, though a superlatively detailed political biography, tells us very little about Wolsey as a man.

The Cardinal is a joint subject with Thomas More and Thomas Cromwell respectively in Jasper Ridley's *'The Statesman and the Fanatic'*, and *'The Cardinal and the Secretary'*.

Any student of Henry VIII will, of course, meet Wolsey in J J Scarisbrick's work of 1968 which still retains its primacy as an account of Henry's reign. For a more modern take, there is Dr David Starkey.

Literature

Wolsey's earliest appearance in literature was in Shakespeare's Henry VIII (believed to be a collaboration between Shakespeare and Fletcher), in which he is shown as scheming to dispatch the Duke of Buckingham and then against Queen Katharine.

Katharine of Aragon disliked Wolsey and Anne Boleyn was his bitterest enemy so, since most of the fiction relating to the period has one or other of them as heroine, Wolsey comes off badly. However that has all changed with Hilary Mantel's novels *'Wolf Hall'* and *'Bring Up the Bodies'*, where her hero, Thomas Cromwell, is shown as being motivated by revenge as he tries to punish those whose ill-treatment of Wolsey, his first master, he resents.

Chapter 15: Thomas Wolsey: Book Review

Wolsey is the subject of one of the earliest biographies ever written, and then a couple of works in the 1970s, including the best academic reference, *'The King's Cardinal'* by Peter Gwyn. The most recent biography of Wolsey is *'Wolsey: The King's Cardinal'*, which we have reviewed here.

Wolsey: The King's Cardinal

Author: John Matusiak

Publisher: The History Press (30 Sept. 2014)

In a nutshell Informative, and makes a clear narrative of complex happenings. Likely to be enjoyed by general readers, rather than academics.

I was looking forward to reading this, as I enjoyed Matusiak's previous work on Henry VIII. One of the things I had liked was his writing style, a little more colourful and individual than just the bald recital of facts that some historians use. However, as time went on, the careful alliterations and the well-chosen adjectives began to pall, and seem over-written and contrived – *'the icy flood of events began to reach the Cardinal's nostrils'*. Maybe simplicity is not such a bad thing!

Matusiak has made much more of an effort than most of Wolsey's biographers to think about Wolsey's internal self. He is shown not just as the proud and vainglorious *'peacock'* but an incredibly hard working perfectionist – unable to delegate, prone to stress-induced illness and bursts of anger when under pressure. Matusiak shows how, the more Wolsey achieved, the more was expected of him – he could never rest.

He had given Henry VIII to think he was invincible and he had to keep delivering.

The author's general style leans towards the sceptical, if not the cynical. Most of the characters presented are shown with all their flaws, and if there is a choice between motives, the less virtuous one tends to be presented. Henry, in particular, is shown as not much more than a conceited buffoon, entirely led by his vanity. There is, of course, some truth in this, but it is only one strand in a multi-layered personality.

Where Matusiak really adds to our knowledge of the Cardinal, is in his early days – the relationship with Henry VII, that so many writers mention only in passing, is filled out, and the development of his working partnership with Richard Foxe, Bishop of Winchester. He also disagrees, with excellent reasoning, with Peter Gwyn whose biography of Wolsey is the standard work of reference, on the importance of Wolsey's time working for the Deputy Lieutenant of Calais, Sir Richard Nanfan. Matusiak shows how this experience equipped Wolsey for his later administrative roles.

He also demonstrates that the idea that Wolsey aspired to be Pope is quite unsupported by the evidence, and that much of our view of Wolsey comes from his enemies, writing after his fall – and that certainly part of his unpopularity with the nobles was based on Wolsey's determination that they should obey the law like lesser men.

It is clear that the author admires Wolsey's cleverness, what contemporaries called his 'angel wit' and his enterprise. No sooner had one scheme failed, than Wolsey would have another in hand. Matusiak also lays out very clearly that in the last great matter, that of the annulment, Henry's actions completely undermined Wolsey, and could well have prevented the grant he so desperately sought.

Overall, Matusiak creates a very clear narrative from a mass of events, and the book is a good guide to Wolsey, although he is much less penetrating when considering the other people of the period, being inclined to repeat old generalisations.

Bibliography

Calendar of State Papers Simancas, British History Online (HMSO, 1892) Hume, Martin A S, ed.,

Calendar of State Papers: Venice <http://www.british-history.ac.uk/cal-state-papers/venice/vol2/vii-lxi> [accessed 7 October 2015]

Letters and Papers, Foreign and Domestic, of the Reign of Henry VIII: Preserved in the Public Record Office, the British Museum, and Elsewhere in England (United Kingdom: British History Online, 2014) https://www.british-history.ac.uk/letters-papers-hen8/ Brewer, John Sherren, and James Gairdner,

Cavendish, George, *Life of Cardinal Wolsey* (Forgotten Books 2009)

Creighton, Mandell, *Cardinal Wolsey* (Bibliolife 28 Jan 2009)

De Lisle, Leanda, *Tudor: The Family Story* (United Kingdom: Chatto & Windus, 2013)

Ellis, Henry, *Original Letters, Illustrative of English History: Including Numerous Royal Letters: From Autographs in the British Museum, the State Paper Office, and One or Two Other Collections.*, 1st edn (New York: Printed for Harding, Triphook, & Lepard, 1824)

Everett, Michael, *The Rise of Thomas Cromwell: Power and Politics in the Reign of Henry VIII 1485 - 1534,* Kindle (New Haven and London: Yale University Press, 2015)

Fletcher, A. and Vernon, L. (1973) *Tudor Rebellions (Seminar Studies in History)*. 2nd edn. Harlow: Longman.

Goodwin, George, *Fatal Rivalry, Flodden 1513: Henry VIII, James IV and the Battle for Renaissance Britain,* ebook (London: Weidenfeld & Nicolson)

Gwyn, Peter, *The King's Cardinal: The Rise and Fall of Thomas Wolsey* (Pimlico 1992)

Hall, Edward, *Hall's Chronicle.* (S.l.: Ams Press, 1909)

Hayward, Maria, ed., *The Great Wardrobe Accounts of Henry VII and Henry VIII* (United Kingdom: London Record Society, 2012)

Holinshed, Raphael, *Holinshed's Chronicles of England, Scotland & Ireland* (United Kingdom: AMS Press, 1997)

Jerdan, William, ed., *Rutland Papers. Original Documents Illustrative of the Courts and Times of Henry VII. and Henry VIII. Selected from the Private Archives of His Grace the Duke of Rutland* (Leopold Classic Library, 2015)

Jones, D. (2014) *The Hollow Crown: The Wars of the Roses and the Rise of The Tudors.* 1st edn. United Kingdom: Faber & Faber Non-Fiction.

Matusiak, John, *Wolsey: The Life of King Henry VIII's Cardinal* (United Kingdom: The History Press Ltd, 2015)

Morse H., *Select Documents Of English Constitutional History,* ed. by George Burton Adams and Morse H Stephens (United States: Kessinger Publishing, 2007)

Reese, Peter, *Flodden: A Scottish Tragedy (Birlinn)* (Edinburgh: Birlinn Publishers, 2003)

Ridley, Jasper, *Statesman and the Fanatic: Thomas Wolsey and Thomas More* London Constable 1982

Scarisbrick, J. J., *Henry VIII (Yale English Monarchs Series)* (Yale University Press 2 April 1997)

Starkey, David, *The Reign of Henry VIII: Personalities and Politics* (Vintage 3 October 2002)

Strickland, A. and Strickland, E. (2011) *Lives of the Queens of England from the Norman Conquest: Volume 3 & 4*. United Kingdom: Cambridge University Press (Virtual Publishing).

Strype, John, *Annals of the Reformation and Establishment of Religion and Other Various Occurrences in the Church of England Etc.* (Oxford: Clarendon Press, 1824),

Vergil, Polydore, *Anglica Historia AD 1485-1637* (Royal Historical, 1950)

Tremlett, G. (2010) *Catherine of Aragon: Henry's Spanish Queen*. London: Faber and Faber.

Weir, Alison, *Henry VIII: King and Court* (London: Jonathan Cape, 2001)

Whitelock, A. (2010) *Mary Tudor: princess, bastard, queen*. 1st edn. New York: Random House Publishing Group.

Williams, Neville, *Henry VIII and His Court*. (London: Littlehampton Book Services, 1971)

Williams, Neville, *The Cardinal and the Secretary: Thomas Wolsey and Thomas Cromwell* (United States: Macmillan, 1976)

www.tudortimes.co.uk